P9-BYD-578

TOP SECRET

Sean Price

Raintree

Chicago, Illinois

Designed by Michelle Lisseter, Kim Miracle, and Bigtop
Printed in China

11 10 09 08 07
10 9 8 7 6 5 4 3 2 1

**Library of Congress
Cataloging-in-Publication Data**

Library of Congress Cataloging-in-Publication Data

Price, Sean.
  Top secret : spy equipment and the Cold War / Sean Price.
      p. cm. -- (American history through primary sources)
  Includes bibliographical references and index.
  ISBN 1-4109-2417-3 (hc) -- ISBN 1-4109-2428-9 (pb)
  1. Espionage--History--20th century--Juvenile literature. 2.
Espionage--Equipment and supplies--Juvenile literature. I. Title. II.
Series.
  UB270.5.P75 2006
  327.12028'4--dc22

                                        2006010688

13-digit ISBNs
978-1-4109-2417-9 (hardcover)
978-1-4109-2428-5 (paperback)

Acknowledgments
The author and publisher are grateful to the following for permission to reproduce copyright material: Bettmann/Corbis **pp. 11**, **21**, **26**, **27** (top and bottom), **28–29**; Dorling Kindersley, Courtesy of the H. Keith Melton Collection **pp. 10**, **13**, **18**, **22**, **25**; Dorling Kindersley, Courtesy of the Imperial War Museum, London **p. 15** (Geoff Dann); Courtesy of the © International Spy Museum **pp. 6–7**, **17**, **19**, **23**; NASA Headquarters-Greatest Images of NASA **p. 8**; Courtesy of National Archives **p. 9**; Courtesy of the National Security Agency **p. 5**; Reuters/Corbis **p. 25** (Jason Reed).

Cover photograph of a matchbox size camera used during World War II reproduced with permission of Bettmann/Corbis.

Photo research by Tracy Cummins.

The publishers would like to thank Nancy Harris and Joy Rogers for their assistance in the preparation of this book.

Every effort has been made to contact copyright holders of any material reproduced in this book. Any omissions will be rectified in subsequent printings if notice is given to the publishers.

Contents

Cold War Spies   **4**

Spy Gadgets   **6**

Eyes in the Sky   **8**

Say, Cheese!   **10**

Spy Dust and Secret Scopes   **12**

Now You See Them, Now You Don't   **14**

Dead Drops   **16**

Tiny Words, Big Message   **18**

For Your Eyes Only   **20**

Poison Pellets and Lipstick Guns   **22**

How Spies Speak   **24**

Real Spy Stories   **26**

James Bond, Super Spy   **28**

Glossary   **30**

Want to Know More?   **31**

Index   **32**

Some words are printed in bold, **like this**. You can find out what they mean on page 30. You can also look in the box at the bottom of the page where they first appear.

Cold War Spies

Shhhh! Spies are working. You cannot see or hear them. They know how to hide. A spy can be a student. A spy can be a doctor or athlete. A spy can be anyone.

Spies trick people. See this photo? It looks like the official seal of the United States. It is really a listening **device**. A device is a tool that does simple tasks. The **Soviet Union** gave it to the United States as a gift. The Soviet Union is known as Russia today.

The Soviets gave this seal in 1945. Americans hung it in an important U.S. office. The **Soviets** could hear everything that went on there.

At the time, Americans and Soviets were fighting the **Cold War**. This lasted 46 years. The Cold War was a strange conflict. There was little shooting. Instead, both sides relied on spies. Those spies used the equipment shown in these pages. Read on!

Cold War	conflict between the United States and Soviet Union that lasted from 1945 to 1991
device	tool that does simple tasks
Soviet	from the Soviet Union
Soviet Union	country that gave little freedom to ordinary people

Spy Gadgets

Spies pretend to be people who they are not. They also use **gadgets**. Gadgets are small tools that do a special job.

The gadget in this picture looks like a piece of **coal**. Coal is a black or brown rock that burns well. This piece of coal is fake. It was **hollow** (empty inside). It was packed with explosives. A spy would paint the coal to make it look real. The spy placed the coal in large containers at railroads or shipyards. The coal would explode when burned.

Spies were able to secretly place the coal in important enemy locations. When the coal exploded, it could cause a lot of damage. The enemy probably never knew that a secret spy gadget had caused this.

coal black or brown rock that burns well
gadget small tool that does a special job
hollow empty inside

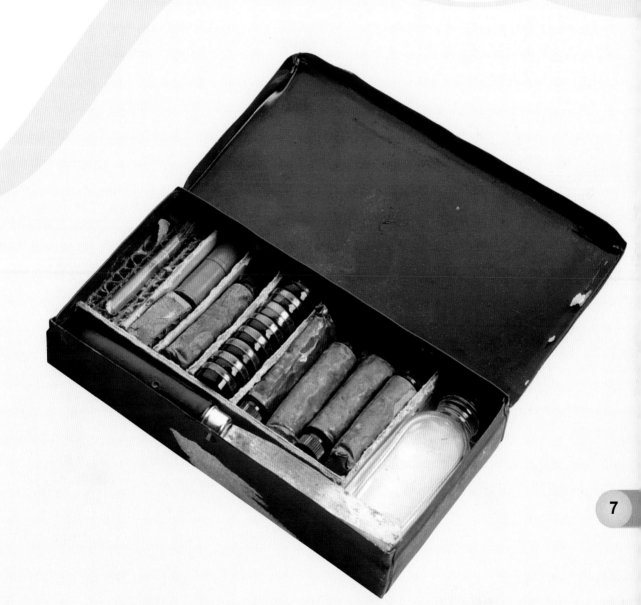

▼ *This picture shows a piece of exploding coal and a paint kit.*

Eyes in the Sky

Both sides in the **Cold War** had weapons. They had **nuclear weapons**. These were bombs that could destroy whole cities in one blast. Everyone feared these weapons. So, both sides tried to keep track of where they were.

The U-2 was the best ▲
spy plane used during
the Cold War.

Early on, the best way to do that was with **spy planes**. A spy plane can take photos as it flies. The most famous spy plane was the U-2. It was flown by U.S. pilots. It flew very high. Other planes could not shoot it down. Its pilots could take more than 4,000 pictures in one flight.

Later, spy **satellites** did an even better job. The spy satellites are very high up in space. They take photos while they circle Earth. They can see well. A spy satellite can read the license plate on a car. Some satellites can even see clearly at night.

▼ Spy satellites take pictures like this from space.

9

nuclear weapon	bomb that can destroy an entire city in one blast
satellites	man-made object that takes photos while it circles Earth
~~spy plane~~	plane that takes photos as it flies

Say, Cheese!

Cold War spies often needed to take photos. But they also needed to keep others from knowing what they were doing. A normal camera was too big. So, scientists created tiny cameras.

Many Cold War spy cameras looked like clothing. Some looked like pieces of jewelry. The one in this picture could be hidden in a tie. The person wearing it snapped the pictures using a button in his pocket.

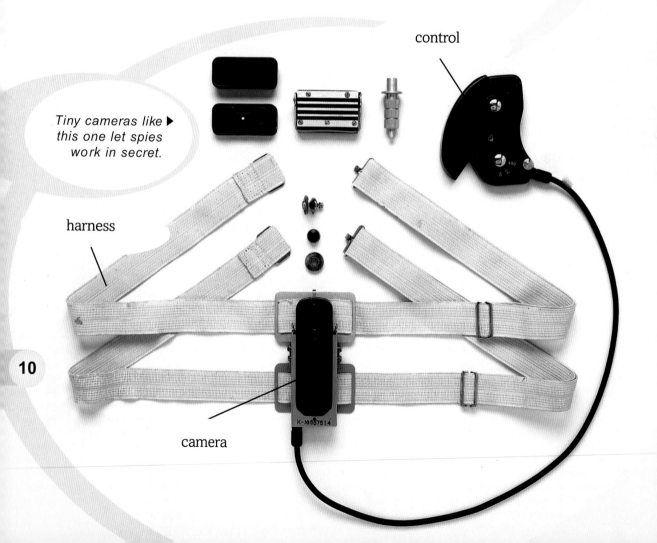

control

Tiny cameras like ▶ this one let spies work in secret.

harness

camera

This spy camera is ▶ so tiny it can fit inside a matchbox.

Cameras could be hidden in other ways. Some were designed to look like pens. Others looked like packs of matches or eyeglasses.

Cameras normally make a clicking noise. But noise can give a spy away. So, spy cameras were made to take pictures silently.

Spy Dust and Secret Scopes

Cold War spies followed people secretly. But it was easy to lose them in a crowd. **Spy dust** solved that problem.

Spy dust was put on a person who was being followed. The dust was invisible to the naked eye. It was also harmless. People never knew they were wearing it. But the dust left a trail. The trail could only be seen under special kinds of light. The spy used that light to follow the dust.

But what happened if a spy tracked someone to a hotel room? How could he know what that person was up to?

A **fiberscope** solved that problem. It is a long tube. It has special glass **fibers**, or threads inside it. These fibers allow it to look under doors. Spies could also drill a hole in a wall. They then poked the fiberscope through the hole.

fiber	thread
fiberscope	tool that uses glass fibers (threads) to look around corners
spy dust	special powder used to track people

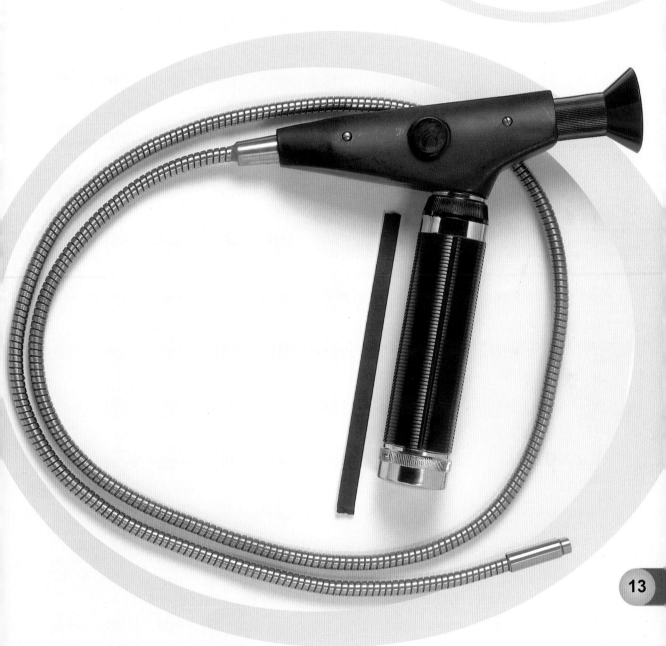

▼This is a fiberscope. It lets spies look under doors and through walls.

13

Now You See Them, Now You Don't

Most **Cold War** spies did not have to change how they looked. They simply fooled people about what they were up to. Yet some spies had to **disguise** (hide) themselves. To do that, they might change their hair color. They might also change their facial features. They might change their clothing. They might wear special make-up.

Disguise is an art. The Central Intelligence Agency (**CIA**) does spying for the United States in other countries. The CIA has experts in disguise. These experts showed Cold War spies how to hide their true **identity** (who they were).

Cold War spies sometimes had to disguise their behavior. In the 1960s, some U.S. spies were given a kit. It let them create many different disguises. One part of the kit was a pair of shoe heels. The heels changed the way the spies walked.

This clothing was a disguise ▶ worn by a British spy named Yvonne Cormeau.

CIA Central Intelligence Agency

Dead Drops

Cold War spies could not be seen with the wrong person. Spies had to be careful whom they talked to. But spies also had to pass on important information. They had to do it secretly.

Dead drops solved this problem. A dead drop is a kind of spy post office. It is a place where one spy can leave items. Spies would leave papers and film. Another spy would come along later and pick them up.

To keep the information safe, many spies used a dead drop **spike**. A spike is a **hollow** tube. It can hold small objects like film. The tube has a pointed end. This allows the spy to hide it by pushing it into the ground.

Garbage cans were sometimes used as dead drops. They were used during the Cold War. Important papers could be made to look like a bag of trash. Only the spy picking up the bag knew the truth.

dead drop   place for spies to leave and pick up information
spike   hollow tube with a pointed end

◄ *This is a photo of a dead drop spike. Spies could hide secret information in it.*

Tiny Words, Big Message

Cold War spies needed smart ways to hide information. One of the best was a **microdot**. A microdot is simply a photograph. It has been made very, very small. In fact, a microdot can be smaller than the period at the end of this sentence. Something so small is easy to sneak past people. It can later be made bigger and be read.

This is a microdot▶ camera. A spy could make a microdot with one of these special cameras.

microdot tiny photograph

Even microdots have to be hidden. They are best hidden in everyday objects. The silver coin in the photo looks like a normal coin. But inside it is **hollow**. There is not much room. But this coin can hide hundreds of microdots. Or it can hide one small piece of paper. Coins like this are still used by spies.

▼ *This hollow silver coin can hide many microdots.*

For Your Eyes Only

Spies sometimes write in **code**. Codes are ways to hide the meaning of a message. They are probably the oldest spy tools. In a code, normal words are replaced by other words or numbers. For instance, "John is thirteen now" could mean, "This factory is building thirteen weapons."

The person sending the message has to know the code. So does the person receiving it. Both sides in the **Cold War** had people working to break codes. They were called **code breakers**. These experts learned to read other people's codes.

Today, code breakers often use computers. They are needed to solve the most difficult codes.

code	way to hide the meaning of a message
code breaker	person who learns to read other people's codes (secret messages)

▼This photo shows spy codes and instructions for using them. Codes let spies speak in secret.

21

Poison Pellets and Lipstick Guns

Cold War spies protected secrets. They often needed weapons to do that. Many clever spy **gadgets** were weapons.

A spy once used an umbrella as a weapon. The spy worked with the **Soviet Union**.

The **Soviets** wanted to kill a man. But they did not want anyone to notice. The spy jabbed the man in the leg with the umbrella's tip. At first, this seemed like an accident. But soon the man became sick and died. A poison **pellet** was found in his leg. A pellet is a tiny ball.

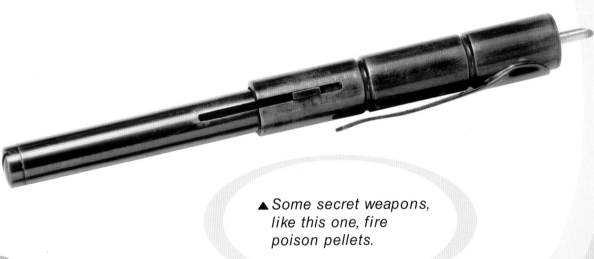

▲ Some secret weapons, like this one, fire poison pellets.

pellet   tiny ball

▼ *This looks like a lipstick case. It is really a gun.*

Other spy weapons produce more of a bang. This lipstick case is called "The Kiss of Death." A spy could turn a knob. This fired a bullet. It was invented by the Soviets. Other spies also used weapons like it.

How Spies Speak

Spies are often hard to spot. Like ghosts, they are not supposed to be noticed. They have their own language. Some words they use are just clever terms. Others help them hide what they are really talking about.

agent	spy
babysitter	bodyguard
Camp Swampy	name of the **CIA's** secret training base
cover	false story a spy tells. It hides his or her real **identity** (who the person is).
double agent	spy who pretends to work for one side. Secretly, he or she works for the other. Also called a "mole."
FBI	Federal Bureau of Investigation. This group hunts for foreign spies hiding in the United States.
flaps and seals	science of secretly opening envelopes and packages
handler	spy's boss
KGB	initials of the top **Soviet** spy organization
music box	secret radio used for sending spy messages
wizard	scientist or other **gadget** expert. The CIA often asked wizards to come up with new gadgets.

▼The CIA sent spies overseas for the United States. They did this during the Cold War.

This is a KGB badge. The ▶ KGB controlled spies for the Soviet Union.

25

Real Spy Stories

Spying for the Soviets

Christopher Boyce became a spy in 1975. He was 22 years old. He and a friend decided to sell U.S. secrets. They sold them to the **Soviets**. They wanted to make money. The pair was caught in 1977. Both went to prison for a long time.

Spying for the United States

Oleg Penkovsky was a Soviet military spy. In 1960 he began giving Soviet secrets to the United States. Penkovsky gave the United States information on Soviet weapons. He also showed how Soviet spies worked. This information helped U.S. spies. Penkovsky was caught in 1962. The Soviets killed him for his actions.

◄This photo shows some of the spy **gadgets** used by Penkovsky.

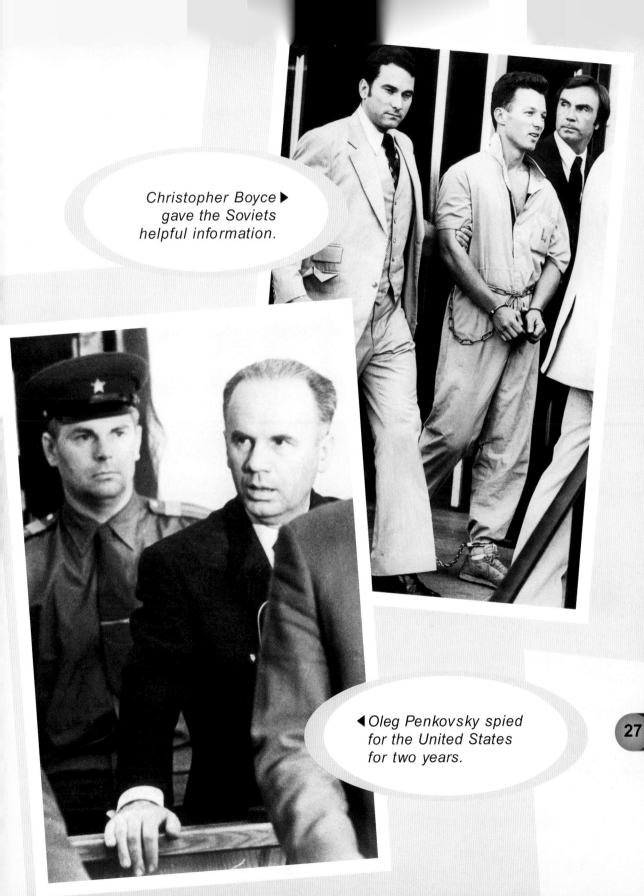

Christopher Boyce ▶
gave the Soviets
helpful information.

◀Oleg Penkovsky spied
for the United States
for two years.

James Bond, Super Spy

Thousands of men and women worked as spies during the **Cold War**. The best-known spy was **fictional**. This means he was a made-up character. His name was Bond. James Bond. His **code** name was 007.

James Bond movies are famous for their spy **gadgets**. Bond's watch might be a super-magnet. His cars always had rockets and guns.

James Bond was created by a British writer. The writer's name was Ian Fleming. Fleming was a real spy. He used some of his own adventures to create Bond. But Fleming's stories are much too wild to be true. Bond always saves the world at the last minute. Usually some gadget helps him do it. In real life, spying is seldom that exciting.

James Bond movies remain popular. More than twenty have been finished so far. James Bond movies lasted long after the Cold War ended in 1991.

James Bond movies▶ have thrilled millions of people.

fictional made up

Glossary

CIA Central Intelligence Agency. This group spies for the United States in other countries.

coal black or brown rock that burns well

code way to hide the meaning of a message

code breaker person who learns to read other people's codes (secret messages)

Cold War conflict between the United States and Soviet Union that lasted from 1945 to 1991

dead drop place for spies to leave and pick up information

device tool that does simple tasks

disguise to change clothing or looks in an attempt to hide one's identity

fiber thread

fiberscope tool that uses special glass fibers (threads) to look around corners

fictional made up

gadget small tool that does a special job

hollow empty inside

identity who someone is

microdot tiny photograph

nuclear weapon bomb that can destroy an entire city in one blast

pellet tiny ball

Soviet from the Soviet Union

Soviet Union country that gave little freedom to ordinary people. It broke up into 15 separate nations in 1991. The biggest of them is Russia.

spike hollow tube with a pointed end

spy dust special powder used to track people

spy plane plane that takes photos as it flies

spy satellite man-made object that takes photos while it circles Earth

Want to Know More?

Books to read

- Burgan, Michael. *Spying and the Cold War*. Chicago: Raintree, 2006.

- Rimington, Dame Stella. *Spies*. Boston: Kingfisher, 2004.

Websites

- http://www.spymuseum.org/index.asp
  Visit the International Spy Museum. Check out this website to learn more about the secret world of spies.

- http://www.cia.gov/cia/information/artifacts/index.htm
  Visit the Central Intelligence Agency (CIA) Museum website to find out more about the CIA and spy gadgets.

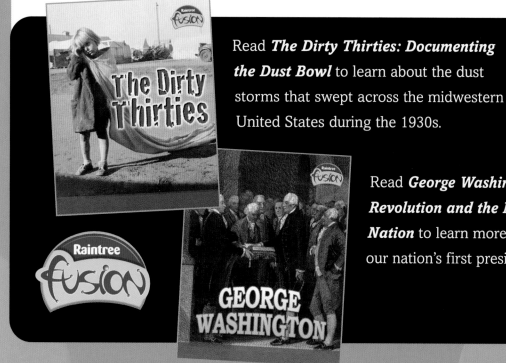

Read ***The Dirty Thirties: Documenting the Dust Bowl*** to learn about the dust storms that swept across the midwestern United States during the 1930s.

Read ***George Washington: Revolution and the New Nation*** to learn more about our nation's first president.

Index

agents 24

babysitters 24

Bond, James 28–29

Boyce, Christopher 26, 27

cameras 10–11, 18

Camp Swampy 24

CIA 14, 24, 25

codes 20–21, 28

Cold War 4, 8, 10, 12, 14, 16,
    18, 20, 22, 25, 28

covers 24

dead drops 16–17

disguises 14–15

double agents 24

explosives 6, 7

FBI 24

fibers 12

fiberscopes 12, 13

fictional spies 28

flaps and seals 24

Fleming, Ian 28

gadgets 6–7, 10–11, 12, 13, 22,
    24, 26, 28

handlers 24

identities 14, 24

KGB 24, 25

listening devices 4, 5

microdots 18–19

music box 24

nuclear weapons 8, 9

Penkovsky, Oleg 26, 27

Soviet Union 4, 22, 23, 24, 25, 26

spies 4, 6, 10, 12, 14, 16, 17, 18,
    20, 22, 24–25, 26–27, 28

spy dust 12

spy planes 8, 9

spy satellites 8, 9

spy weapons 22–23

United States 4, 8, 14, 24, 25, 26

wizards 24